*Quick*GUIDES

everything you need to know...fast

Newsletter
Autumn/Winter 2003

mer seems to hav...
e UK – subjects a...
oughly enjoyable...
urse got good view...
ry special indeed.

The summer craft shows...
have loved meeting old friends and talki...
busy pre-Christmas line-up of shows. Come and...
News from Bandhavgarh is an emotional mix. There...
but good news of the three litters of cubs that I had superb view...
Thank you for the many kind comments about my book, wh...
Harrods stock it! And now is the time of year to launch...
Christmas and next year!
...pe to see you in the...

Newsletters

...icle on the main road.
inside a tourist jeep and attacked the two French passengers.
Probably because of her internal injuries and the lack of teeth
(knocked out in the road collision) she was not able to inflict
life-threatening wounds. After a few minutes she left the jeep
and disappeared into the forest. Bachchi has not been seen
since and we are now sure that she has died from her injuries.
She was the first tiger that I ever saw and in recent years her
family have become the dominant tigers of Bandhavgarh. An
elusive tigress and a superb mother of eight cubs, Bachchi
will be greatly missed.
Immediately after her disappearance, concern turned to
r three sub-adult cubs and how they would fare. In August I
ard the wonderful news that two of the cubs, a male and
nale, were regularly seen and very much hunting fo...
themselves (in late June the third cub had...
porcupine quills). The future look...
Bachchi's female cub...
same area...

Newsletter

by Jill Ritchie
reviewed by Jinny Gender

WIREMILL
PUBLISHING LTD

Across the world the organizations and institutions that fundraise to finance their work are referred to in many different ways. They are charities, non-profits or not-for-profit organizations, non-governmental organizations (NGOs), voluntary organizations, academic institutions, agencies, etc. For ease of reading, we have used the term Nonprofit Organization, Organization or NPO as an umbrella term throughout the *Quick* Guide series. We have also used the spellings and punctuation used by the author.

Published by
Wiremill Publishing Ltd.
Edenbridge, Kent TN8 5PS, UK
info@wiremillpublishing.com
www.wiremillpublishing.com
www.quickguidesonline.com

British Library Cataloguing in Publication Data
A catalogue record for this book is available from the British Library.

ISBN Number 1-905053-01-0

Printed by Rhythm Consolidated Berhad, Malaysia
Cover Design by Jennie de Lima and Edward Way
Design by Colin Woodman

Disclaimer of Liability
The author, reviewer and publisher shall have neither liability nor responsibility to any person or entity with respect to any loss or damage caused or alleged to be caused directly or indirectly by the information contained in this book. While the book is as accurate as possible, there may be errors, omissions or inaccuracies.

CONTENTS

NEWSLETTERS

Introduction

The majority of charities worldwide do not have newsletters. There are many reasons for this including:

- Fear that newsletters will be expensive, time-consuming or complicated.

- No one has the time to write one.

- There is a lack of funding to produce one.

- No one knows how to write/edit/compile a newsletter.

- No one knows what to include in one.

- No one has thought of writing one.

- Or the perception that all of the above are true whether or not they are.

Not understanding the value of having a newsletter may also result in an organisation's members feeling that a newsletter is not suitable or necessary for them. Yet, a good newsletter carefully thought through and produced can be a useful part of the communications toolbox for dealing with the public and with the organisation's donors, supporters, volunteers, and staff.

Newsletters need not be fancy. They need not be expensive. They need not be long. In these days of computers and printers, email and inexpensive photocopying, it is often much easier to produce a newsletter simply and quickly than in the days when even relatively simple newsletters had to be typeset and sent to printers.

This guide will help you evaluate whether a newsletter would be useful for your organisation. If the answer is yes, it will then help you plan and produce one.

Why Have a Newsletter?

It is important to understand the uses of a newsletter and then determine which are appropriate for your organisation. They include:

- Communicating to the organisation's support base and other potential supporters

- Informing people about your organisation and its work

- Encouraging people to visit your Web site

- Keeping the name of your organisation in the thoughts of supporters

- Highlighting selected aspects of your work

- Thanking and acknowledging donors

- Serving as a fundraising tool

- Profiling individual beneficiaries

- Motivating people to action:
  - ❑ To donate
  - ❑ To volunteer
  - ❑ To buy tickets to events
  - ❑ To become members
  - ❑ To encourage bequests

What a Newsletter Should Include

The information included in your newsletter will be determined by its purpose. Depending on what that purpose is, you may want to include some or all of the following:

General information on your organisation and its work

Every newsletter should include information about the organisation and its work. Although it may be the 309th edition of your newsletter, it may be the first copy someone sees. It may also give information about other aspects of your work to supporters or volunteers who are involved with a different area.

If your mission statement is not too long, it may be useful to include it as well to remind everyone what your organisation is working to achieve.

Basic contact details for your organisation including address, mailing address if different, telephone, fax, email, and website.

This is also important to include in each newsletter for those who may be seeing your newsletter for the first time and want to contact your organisation for further information. It is also important because it makes it easy for readers to respond instantly to articles in the newsletter without having to find your contact details.

Names of contact staff and/or governing council

This reminds readers whom they can contact if they have questions or want to become further involved. You want to make it easy for them to find the appropriate people. By including the names of your governing council, readers may recognise friends or colleagues, celebrities or other well-known people who might inspire their interest or involvement.

Up-to-date news and information

Newsletters are a great way to disseminate information about what your organisation has been doing. They allow you to spread the word about staff changes, programme successes, new products for sale and so forth. They keep your readers involved with what's happening with your organisation.

WHAT A NEWSLETTER SHOULD INCLUDE

LOTS OF PHOTOGRAPHS

Pictures are still worth a thousand words. They provide a visible illustration of your stories. They also give you the opportunity to show celebrities attending your events, volunteers enjoying their work for your organisation, or the beneficiaries of your activities benefiting from your work. Ensure that you have captions for your photographs and that you correctly identify the people in them.

Reviewer's Comment

Ensure you obtain permission from people in photographs to use their names. This also gives you the opportunity to ensure you have their names correctly spelled.

INFORMATION ABOUT FUNDRAISING INITIATIVES AND EVENTS

This is an easy way to let your readers know about upcoming fundraising activities. It can tell them about past successes and thank those who were involved with them. You may also want to provide forms for readers to request tickets to events or to ask for further information about membership and giving opportunities, gifts at death and so forth.

THANKS AND ACKNOWLEDGMENT OF VOLUNTEERS

The newsletter provides an ideal opportunity to thank those who have been involved in your organisation. You might do this regularly or once or twice a year. It may be part of the newsletter or a special thank-you insert. Everyone likes to see his or her name in print. Crucially don't omit anyone and ensure that you spell each person's name correctly.

PROFILES OF STAFF

Regular profiles of paid staff and volunteers encourage the reader to feel involved with the organisation and the people who work for it. Staff can provide their own biographical sketches, or there could be standard questions answered by each person profiled.

ARTICLES ABOUT YOUR ACTIVITIES

These types of articles will probably form the largest part of your newsletter and rightly so.

Human-interest stories are great. Instead of including articles about the work you do from a theoretical or general perspective, write about how your services have specifically helped people or even turned their lives around.

Continued on Page 8

Don't say, *"We provide over 15 000 meals to the homeless each year as well as provide counselling and practical advice in accessing benefits."*

Rather: *"Meet John Smith, six months after our staff and volunteers met him living on the streets. Now he has been reunited with his son with whom he had lost contact. John is living in his own accommodation and is attending a woodworking-training course put on by our organisation in connection with the local craft market. In fact, he is already selling wooden toys after only six weeks on the course and has also sold his work to two local shops. It is only through the generosity of our donors and the selfless help of our volunteers that we can continue to help people like John."*

Also, with his permission, a photograph of John and his products should be included.

Include stories about the beneficiaries of your work such as that illustrated above. Does your organisation provide life-changing or life-enhancing services? Does your school have a special story about a special student? Are you saving an endangered species? Readers love success stories. Donors love success stories. The great things they read about in your newsletter should motivate them to contribute toward additional successes.

Ensure that you are not breaking any privacy laws by featuring people without their permission. In many countries, this applies to naming and/or photographing children.

Even if your beneficiaries are animals, endangered wildlife or rain forests, students, theatres or some other organisation, you can easily feature people in your articles. After all, it's people who devote time and energy to making a difference in the lives of animals or in the saving of fauna and flora facing extinction.

You don't want your newsletter to include:

INAPPROPRIATE ARTICLES FOR YOUR READERSHIP

Articles should be tailored to your readers. If your newsletter is being sent to supporters of your organisation and not colleagues or others in similar endeavours, the newsletter is probably not the best place to have highly technical articles or articles that would not be enjoyed by the majority of readers. If your newsletter is sent to a broad constituency, it can be segmented into sections appropriate for the various groups who will see it.

The newsletter is not the best place to indulge the editor or contributors with materials of interest to them but not to the majority of readers. Stick to the subject, and to the purpose of the newsletter, which is to promote the interests of the organisation.

In no event should articles be boring or badly written.

LONG ARTICLES

Generally your newsletter should be "newsy" and easy to read. Long articles, like technical articles, are generally best left to more scholarly or other type of publication. Unless, of course, they are appropriate for the style of newsletter you have determined is appropriate for your organisation.

ANYTHING THAT SHOULD BE USED FOR INTERNAL COMMUNICATION ONLY

The results of a staff football match, a photo of the secretary's new baby or the winner of an internal lucky draw are generally not of interest to anyone not employed at the nonprofit organisation (NPO). Keep this type of information for the staff room or internal message board.

Newsletters don't have to fit within any particular style. Many newsletters are written in a light and easy-to-read style. This doesn't detract from the seriousness of the organisation's mission or its work but encourages readers to look at the newsletter and read the various sections. Other newsletters are written in a more formal style, particularly if they will be distributed both to the general public and to specific professional readers.

When writing an informal type of newsletter, sentences should be kept short, preferably not exceeding 18–20 words. Also, paragraphs should not be too long — they will look too intimidating to plough through. Five to six sentences per paragraph are usually sufficient.

It's been said that *if* you know the rules, you can break them. This applies to grammar and to style of language. Many newsletters are written in a chatty, almost conversational style that works very well both for the readers and for the writers. Others find that a slightly more formal style works in the context of their organisation and those involved in the production of the newsletter. There are no hard and fast rules.

Every style will be different, but the following hints will help those unused to writing this type of publication:

■ Avoid jargon. Many of your readers won't understand what you mean when you use words unfamiliar to them. You won't impress them with how efficient the organisation is. You'll just turn them off from reading the next newsletter.

■ Don't waffle. There is no need to write more than you need to. When you've said what you need to say, stop.

■ Keep language simple. Simple language is far more effective and ensures that all your readers understand what is being said.

■ Avoid generalisations and give facts. Don't say, "Over the years we have helped thousands of homeless people turn their lives around." Rather, "In the 15 years since a group of concerned citizens started Heaven Shelters, 27,000 homeless people have … " Be specific.

LANGUAGE AND STYLE

■ Be careful of the terminology you use. One can so easily and inadvertently offend people. If you are uncertain what to say or how to say it, ask the advice of staff members within the organisation who are familiar with the terminology in their areas of work.

Use *"we"* and *"you"* because they involve the reader more directly. Instead of *"the AIDS pandemic will continue unabated unless it is addressed,"* you may write, *"it is only through the efforts of organisations such as ours and your loyal support that we will halt the AIDS pandemic."*

As in public speaking, good article writing should "hook" a reader with an opening line that is both catchy and brief. The first sentence should create sufficient interest for the reader to want to know more. Newspapers also put their most catchy information in the headlines and then make the first sentence of an article enticing enough to prompt one to read on.

The language and style of the newsletter need to work for you, but there is no rule that requires a newsletter to be internally consistent. The fundraising department may produce a fun, casual page with lots of pictures of events, volunteers and contests, while a programme department may produce a serious article about a need that is being addressed. The director of the organisation can write in his or her own style.

Reviewer's Comment
One can't stress enough the need to make your style fit your organisation and your culture. If in doubt, look at other newsletters produced by organisations around you, or ask colleagues and some recipients how they react to certain styles.

CONTRIBUTORS OF ARTICLES

The fact that a newsletter will contain a range of articles, regular materials and reports means that many people can be involved in its writing and production.

Contributors can include:

STAFF MEMBERS WHO ARE RESPONSIBLE FOR REPORTING ON THE WORK OF THEIR DEPARTMENTS.
A fundraising department may be enthusiastic to provide a constant stream of donor information and opportunities, while other departments may require encouragement to share information with readers.

STAFF MEMBERS WHO ARE RESPONSIBLE FOR OBTAINING INFORMATION FROM OTHERS IN THE ORGANISATION AND PREPARING ARTICLES FROM THAT INFORMATION.
These may be individuals with a particular interest in writing, a particular skill in interviewing, or a job dedicated to producing the newsletter or newsletter articles.

VOLUNTEERS WHO PARTICIPATED IN AN EVENT OR PROGRAMME FOR THE NPO AND ARE WRITING ABOUT THEIR EXPERIENCE OF THE EVENT OR PROGRAMME.
Choose those who have had a good experience working with you. It is much more effective to have volunteers talking about the good work of the organisation and how much they enjoyed the experience.

STAFF MEMBERS WHO PROVIDE THE SERVICES OF THE ORGANISATION.
The staff member who looks after the abused dogs that are brought into the shelter, the nurse who works with the elderly patients, the teacher, anyone delivering services can write powerfully of their experiences.

BENEFICIARIES OF THE WORK OF THE ORGANISATION.
Beneficiaries should be encouraged to share their experiences and particularly the benefit they receive from the organisation. Only parents who have lost a child can truly express their grief, only a homeless person can really write about life on the streets, and only a counsellor who spends his or her days talking to people with terminal illness can really know the impact of his or her work. Writing by beneficiaries can be very powerful. Beneficiaries are, after all, what the organisation is all about.

A Calendar of Events

Always have upcoming events featured in your newsletter.

This gives the fundraising department an opportunity to alert readers of fundraising activities and gives readers an opportunity to consult their diaries and decide which events to attend. It also can give publicity for other departments of the organisation that organise events, even if the events are professional ones such as technical conferences or seminars.

It also provides readers with information about events related to the activities of the organisation – conferences organised by it for others in the same field, a launch of a new programme to save an endangered species, publication dates for new books by or about the organisation, unveiling of new art on the premises or the opening of a new wing of a hospital.

All these events, even if they are not open to the public, tell your readers that you are actively doing work and to look out for public mention of the activity.

Having a calendar in your newsletters puts pressure on you to send your newsletter out on time. It can be very frustrating for a reader to receive a newsletter containing a calendar with events that have already occurred.

Ensure that your readers have a simple way to respond to events listed on your calendar. If they need to book, give the information about whom to contact. If they can just turn up on the day, that should also be made clear to readers.

LAYOUT

You need to determine what your newsletter will look like. Will it mirror other publications from your organisation or stand alone? The first ensures that the newsletter is seen as part of the organisation's stable of materials. The second gives the newsletter designer the freedom to design something that will specifically work as a newsletter for the organisation.

There are numerous computer programmes that will assist in the design of newsletters. They are particularly useful for organisations that don't have easy access to designers or the funds to spend on a special design.

Those involved in planning a newsletter should look at other newsletters, either printed or Web versions, to see what else is available and to choose the design elements that are best for their own needs.

After the general design has been determined, the specific layout of the newsletter should be considered.

Decisions to be made include:

- The number of pages the newsletter will contain
- The typeface to be used
- Whether there will be regularly occurring columns or articles that will appear in each edition
- Whether there will be regular contributors
- The number of columns per page
- Headline style or styles
- General layout of the articles
- Photographs, sketches and diagrams
- Colour and type of paper
- Page numbering, indexing, table of contents

Again, it can be useful to look at existing newsletters when deciding how to structure the look of your publication.

LAYOUT

TYPEFACE

Consider the typeface carefully.
Experiment and have fun doing so,
but consider:

- Is the typeface reader-friendly?
  Not all are. Ask a professional if you
  are uncertain.

- Will the typeface look good when
  used with a lot of text?
  Test it and see what you think. Ask
  colleagues for their opinion.

- Does the organisation have a
  standard typeface used across all
  its publications that you either want
  to use or must use?
  Find out the requirements.

- Will the publication be sent by
  e-mail? Typefaces sometimes don't
  work in different computer
  programmes.

The simpler or more standard the
typeface, the more likely it is to work
on the greatest number of computers.

HEADLINES

Headlines can make or break a
newsletter.

Look at newspapers and magazines and
their headlines for ideas of which ones
are interesting, which ones grab your
attention and which ones are boring.

Excellent ones make you want to read
the article. Bad ones make people
want to turn the page. Don't ignore
them while focussing on the text of an
article. Both headlines and
subheadings require careful attention.

Headlines for newsletters sent by
e-mail can be handled in two ways.
They can either be like traditional
headlines with an article following or
they can stand on their own and, when
clicked on, send the reader to the
appropriate article. Either way, they still
fulfil the function of engaging the
interest of the readers and making
them want to read the article.

A concept worth considering is having a theme for each newsletter.

This could be as simple as using the time of year as the theme or organising a newsletter around a particular event (the unveiling of a painting) or issue (a particular programme or need of the organisation).

For example, an NPO concerned with domestic animals might select pet adoption as its theme.

The newsletter might be organised as follows:

- The front cover might have a picture of a happy adoptive pet with its new family.

- One article might focus on the need for adoption.

- Another article might focus on the adoption programme that the organisation runs and its success, and include interviews with families who are happy with the pets they have adopted.

- Yet another article might ask for donations specifically for this programme.

- Pictures of an event could highlight those of celebrities and their adopted pets.

- A "Letters to the Editor" column could include a number of letters from participants in the pet-adoption programme.

Find out what discounts may be available to your organisation. In many places, there are discounts on bulk mailing. Some countries have NPO rates while others allow a reduced price if envelopes have been sorted and bundled according to postal codes. Investigate the situation in your country in order to maximise any money-saving opportunities with regard to postage.

You will also have to determine who will put newsletters into envelopes, affix labels and stamps, and sort and bundle the envelopes. Staff or volunteers can do these tasks, or you may find that using a mailing house is cost-effective.

FREQUENCY

The question of how often a newsletter should be produced often causes concern or confusion. There is no one-size-fits-all answer to this. The frequency of a newsletter (ranging from monthly to annually) depends on a number of factors such as how much you have to say, how much time you have, and what funds you have to cover the costs. On average, charities write two to four newsletters each year, but there are no fixed rules to this. You know that you have your timing right when people contact you should a new edition be overdue!

Reviewer's Comment

Ensure you do everything possible to discover if recipients move so you don't waste time and money sending newsletters that never arrive. Different places have different rules regarding forwarding of mail or the ability to obtain address-change information.

THE CRITICAL PATH (TO-DO LIST)

Prepare a critical path (a to-do list with deadlines) and work backward from the final date. The following is an example of the contents of a critical path for a newsletter to which dates should be added:

- Hold planning session and finalise article selection and people responsible for each article.

- Notify all contributors of articles, number of words and deadline for copy.

- Editor receives copy.

- Editing is completed.

- Photographs are planned and assigned or identified from stock.

- Photographs are received.

- Meet with data-processing/layout/ typesetting person (or sit down at the computer and put all of the information together into the appropriate format).

- Put the newsletter together on the computer or produce hard copy for the printer or typesetter.

- Proofread the draft.

- Make changes.

- Proofread the final draft.

- Sign off on draft or give go-ahead to printer (or print from your computer).

- Newsletters are delivered from printer.

- Newsletters are placed into envelopes.

- Envelopes are taken to post office.

Simply by compiling a critical path, you will establish the necessary deadlines crucial for the success of your newsletter. You will also be able to determine when you will need to begin each newsletter and how much time you will have for each newsletter's writing and production.

Hard Copy or Email?

With the advent of the Internet, many NPOs have switched to communicating with their target audience electronically. However, it is not a straightforward matter of simply switching overnight from mailing a printed copy of a newsletter to merely sending out newsletters by e-mail.

It is best to approach the potential of sending out newsletters electronically with caution. It is usually far cheaper than producing a printed newsletter and can achieve the same results if handled with care. However, there are negatives attached to electronic newsletters.

Some questions to ask yourself when deciding whether to make the switch:

■ Do your readers have computers or access to computers?

■ Are they computer-literate?

■ What computer programme will you use and will be accessible to all your readers?

■ Will your newsletter be part of an e-mail or will it be sent as an attachment?

■ Will readers' computers reject attachments?

■ Will you need a specialist's assistance in producing an electronic newsletter?

■ Will you be able to use photographs or will they make the attachment too large for readers to download?

■ Will readers value something that comes as an e-mail or e-mail attachment as much as something that comes in the mail?

In order to set about making the switch from printed newsletters sent out by post to those sent out in electronic format, begin by separating recipients into various groups. Start with regular donors and supporters. Ask their permission via the regular mail to change to e-mail.

Continued on page 20

HARD COPY OR E-MAIL?

You might try a communication such as *"As a regular supporter, we feel that you will share our thinking about the cost savings we can make in our administration, thus allowing more funds to be used for programmes. One area is reducing the amount of materials we send in the mail and communicating instead by e-mail. May we communicate with you by e-mail in the future? If so, kindly let us have your e-mail address."* Or *"As our partners in the work we do, we believe that you, too, share our concerns about spending on administration. In the interest of saving money to better serve our beneficiaries, may we communicate with you electronically in the future?"*

You could include a reply coupon in your next mailing for people to complete and return, or you could ask them to e-mail their response should they be happy to receive e-mails from you. Also, have your Web site adapted so people can request that electronic newsletters be sent to them. (Don't forget to archive past newsletters on your Web site.)

You could also ask your regular supporters to forward the electronic newsletters to selected friends who may find them interesting.

It is important that your newsletter not be regarded as spam either by the recipients or by the authorities in your country. It is vital to investigate the legislation (if any) in your country pertaining to spam and to follow the rules.

Reviewer's Comment
I receive an e-newsletter (electronic newsletter) that has various TOPICS in bold and a paragraph about that topic. Then if I am interested in that topic, I click on the title for the whole article. This is great, although it may be a bit sophisticated for electronic-newsletter novices.

It would also be great if the electronic newsletter could send the reader directly to a place on the NPO's Web site that can accept donations by credit card to make support as easy as possible.

COSTS AND ADVERTISING

The cost of producing a newsletter will depend on all the elements associated with the newsletter. If it's printed and mailed, it could include:

- An editor or other organiser of the newsletter
- Writers
- Photographers
- Designer
- Typesetter
- Printer
- Envelopes
- Stamps/postage
- Mailing house or "stuffers"

Costs of an e-mail newsletter will include:

- Editor
- Writers
- Photographers
- Computer designer
- Computer operator
- Company that sends out e-mails or a programme that will do it for you.

You will need to evaluate how much you can afford to spend, how much you are willing to spend, and what product you can produce for that amount.

ADVERTISING

One way of deferring the costs of producing a newsletter is to seek advertising from commercial companies. Be careful to ensure that the advertising does not irritate readers and that it complements the work of the organisation or at least does not detract from it.

Local businesses may be interested in advertising in a local organisation's newsletter, while larger companies may be more attracted to a newsletter with a larger readership.

In some cases, advertising may not be appropriate. It may be inappropriate for an advertisement to appear next to a serious article. Or, an advertisement might clash with a sponsored event if the event sponsor and advertiser are competitors.

It may be possible for a newsletter itself to be sponsored by one company rather than seeking advertisements from many. The sponsor could even change from edition to edition.

Evaluate the costs of procuring sponsorship or advertising against the financial benefits of having it.

It is important to evaluate the benefit of the newsletter in light of the cost and time spent in producing it. Any responses from the newsletter should be kept and noted. These may include bookings for events, purchases of items advertised in the newsletter, or donations received as a result of someone reading an edition.

Complaints should not only be kept but should also be acted upon. A complaint should be seen as a benefit because the person took the time to make it.

Numbers of complaints indicate you've misjudged something among your readers. The odd complaint can be dealt with by responding directly to the person making the complaint.

Ensure that any communication received in response to your newsletter is sent to the specific department or author.

Compliments as well as complaints can be extremely valuable both in evaluating the success of the newsletter, its style and format and in evaluating how the newsletter is supporting the general activities of your organisation.

Reviewer's Comment

You might consider putting a response card in your newsletter from time to time to elicit general responses as well as specific information. You might, for example, ask readers what articles had been read or which features they had enjoyed. Readers of e-newsletters could be asked whether they were able to access all the items on their computer.

FINAL THOUGHTS

Newsletters can be a useful communication tool and source of information for a range of people connected to an NPO. As with all materials produced by an NPO, the desired objectives need to be carefully considered, the style and content discussed in order to achieve those objectives, and cost and time implications considered.

A good newsletter, well written and produced, can be an excellent advertisement for your NPO. It need not be expensive, but it needs to be appropriate for the organisation, its size and activities.

Increasingly newsletters are not produced in printed versions but are sent by electronic means. This may provide an opportunity for organisations without extensive resources to produce e-mail newsletters that meet the objective of communication without extensive cost.

JILL RITCHIE

Jill Ritchie started her own business at the age of 18 while also studying. By the time she was 28, she had created jobs for 120 people in a factory with seven retail outlets. At the same time, she was spending more time doing voluntary charity work than anything else. She then closed her business and entered the NPO sector as a member of the start-up team of the Triple Trust, the highly successful South African job-creation organisation, where she initially trained trainers and ran the organisation's marketing arm. After a year there, she took over the fundraising and, in five years, took the Triple Trust from a budget of South African Rand 100,000 per annum to Rand 9 million, most of which was raised from northern hemisphere donors. Jill left to start her own fundraising consultancy and book-publishing business, which she has run for the past 15 years. She has edited three books and written 15, 12 on fundraising, of which the best known is *Fundraising for the New Millennium.*

She has arranged numerous successful events for South African NPOs, raising both funds and friends for the organisations in the process. She has achieved much success in the field of cause-related marketing.

Jill is Vice President of the Southern Africa Institute of Fundraising and also heads up its Ethics Committee. She is in demand around the world as a speaker on fundraising.

Jinny Gender, Reviewer

Jinny Gender has a degree in sociology from Lindenwood College in St. Charles, Missouri. In a nonprofit career spanning 30 years, Jinny has served on dozens of nonprofit boards – as president of many – and worked tirelessly as a volunteer. Missouri Governor Mel Carnahan appointed her to the Missouri Board of Social Workers in 1994 where she was the first public member ever.

In the last 10 years alone, Jinny has served on 20 nonprofit boards including: National Public Radio KWMU in St. Louis, past president; Metro St. Louis Women's Political Caucus, past president; ALIVE, Alternatives to Living in Violent Environments, past president; Lindenwood Alumni Club, past president; Charter board member of the St. Louis County Shelter for Abused Women; Confluence, St. Louis; Magic House, Museum for Children; and Y.E.S., Youth Emergency Service. She has been a hearing tester for the Special School district for 20 years and has had her own weekly talk-radio show on station WGNU in St. Louis for the last 10 years. With a partner, Jinny Gender has her own consulting business, International Charity Consultants.